Families

Grandparents

Revised Edition

Rebecca Rissman

Heinemann Library
Chicago, Illinois

www.capstonepub.com
Visit our website to find out more information about Heinemann-Raintree books.

To order:
Phone 800-747-4992
Visit www.capstonepub.com to browse our catalog and order online.

© 2011, 2021 Heinemann Library
an imprint of Capstone Global Library, LLC
Chicago, Illinois

All rights reserved. No part of this publication may be reproduced or transmitted in any form or by any means, electronic or mechanical, including photocopying, recording, taping, or any information storage and retrieval system, without permission in writing from the publisher.

Edited by Rebecca Rissman and Catherine Veitch
Designed by Ryan Frieson
Picture research by Tracy Cummins
Originated by Capstone Global Library Ltd

Library of Congress Cataloging-in-Publication Data is available on the Library of Congress website.
ISBN 9781484668320 (pb)

Acknowledgments
We would like to thank the following for permission to reproduce photographs: Getty Images: aldomurillo, cover, Alex Mares-Manton, 18, Ariel Skelley, 21, Don Mason, 12, 23, Image Source, 17, Jupiterimages, 9, Kevin Dodge, 14, Kristy-Anne Glubish, 20, Nils Hendrik Muller, back cover, 19, Ron Levine, 16; iStockphoto: Ann Marie Kurtz, 5, Diane Labombarbe, 22; Shutterstock: bbernard, 7, bearinmind, 4, 23, Mehmet Dilsiz, 6, Monkey Business Images, 10, 11, 13, 23, NDAB Creativity, 8, Yarek Gora, 15

We would like to thank Anne Pezalla and Nancy Harris for their invaluable help in the preparation of this book.

Every effort has been made to contact copyright holders of any material reproduced in this book. Any omissions will be rectified in subsequent printings if notice is given to the publisher.

Printed in the United States 5961

Contents

What Is a Family? 4

What Are Families Like? 8

Who Are Grandparents? 10

Different Grandparents 12

Family Tree 22

Picture Glossary 23

Index 24

What Is a Family?

A family is a group of people who care for each other.

People in a family are different ages.

All families are different.

All families are special.

What Are Families Like?

Some families like to play games.

Some families like to cook together.

Who Are Grandparents?

Some families have parents. Parents are adults who have children.

Parents have parents, too!
They are called grandparents.

Different Grandparents

Your parent's mother is your grandmother.

Your parent's father is your grandfather.

Some families have
many grandparents.

Some families have few grandparents. Some families do not have any grandparents.

Some grandparents live far from their families.

Some grandparents live with their families.

Some grandparents care for their grandchildren.

Some grandchildren help care for their grandparents.

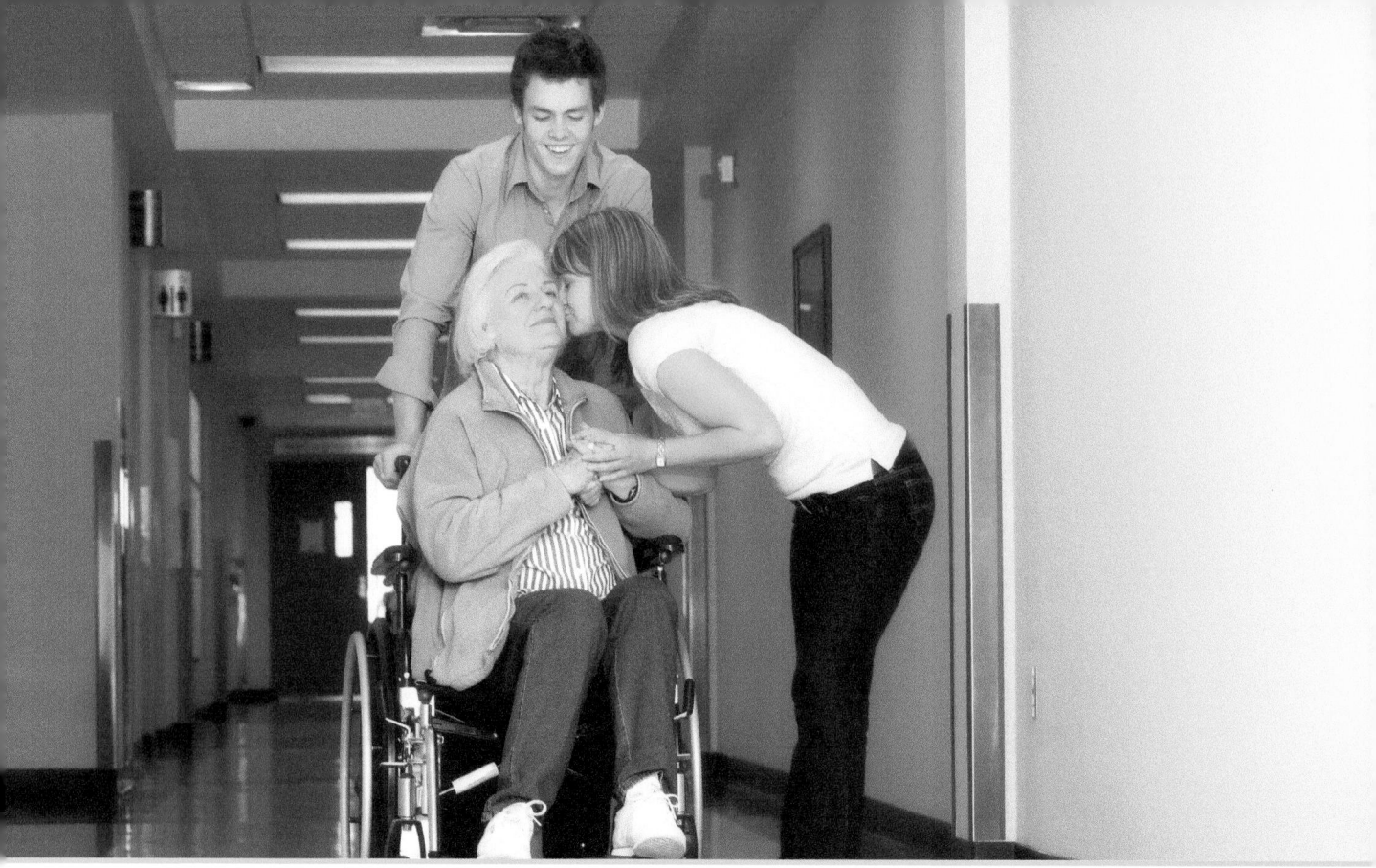

Some families visit their grandparents at special homes.

Do you have grandparents?

Family Tree

Grandmother
Grandfather
Grandmother
Grandfather
Mother
Father
You

Picture Glossary

grandfather your parent's father

grandmother your parent's mother

parent adult who has children

Index

grandfather 13, 22
grandmother 12, 22
grandparent 11, 14, 15, 16, 17, 18, 19, 20, 21, 22
parent 10, 11, 12, 13, 22

Note to Parents and Teachers

Before Reading

Explain to children that people in families are often related to each other. Most children are related to their parents. And parents have parents, too! They are a child's grandparents!

After Reading

Ask children if they have special nicknames for their grandparents, such as Grammy or Papa. Make a list of these names on the board.